LIZARDS AND SALAMANDERS

BY MARTHA LONDON

Published by The Child's World®
1980 Lookout Drive • Mankato, MN 56003-1705
800-599-READ • www.childsworld.com

Photographs ©: JD Carballo/Shutterstock Images, cover (lizard), 2, 11, 20, 24 (lizard); Federico Crovetto/Shutterstock Images, cover (salamander), 3, 16, 20, 24 (salamander); Tanes Ngamsom/Shutterstock Images, 5; Shutterstock Images, 6, 17; Gudkov Andrey/Shutterstock Images, 9; Blue Dog Studio/Shutterstock Images, 10; Jay Ondreicka/Shutterstock Images, 13; Tristan Tan/Shutterstock Images, 14; Milan Zygmunt/Shutterstock Images, 19

ISBN 9781503835955
LCCN 2019943063

Printed in the United States of America

ABOUT THE AUTHOR

Martha London is a writer. She lives in Minnesota. When she isn't writing books, you can find her hiking in the woods.

TABLE OF CONTENTS

Cold-Blooded Animal

A **cold-blooded** animal with a long body and tail lies on a rock. It is using the sun to keep itself warm. Is it a lizard or a salamander? How are they different?

Salamanders can be found in many places of the world.

Lizards come in many colors. Some lizards, such as chameleons, can even change their colors.

Lizards

Lizards are **reptiles**. They have sharp claws on their feet. Lizards are not slimy. They have scales. Their scales are dry and rough.

Some lizards are tiny. Others are huge. The biggest lizard is the Komodo dragon. It weighs about 175 pounds (80 kg). The smallest lizard is only 0.75 inches (16 mm) long. It lives on an island in the Caribbean Sea.

Lizards live nearly everywhere in the world. Antarctica is the only **continent** without lizards.

Komodo dragons can only be found in parts of Indonesia.

Many lizards lay eggs with soft shells.

Lizards lay eggs. They dig a hole and bury their eggs.

Most lizards are awake during the day. Lizards need the sun to stay warm. Many lizards lie on rocks. They soak up the sun.

Salamanders

Salamanders are **amphibians**. They live near water. Some spend most of their life in water. Salamanders have wet skin instead of scales. They do not have claws.

Salamanders are amphibians, just like frogs are.

Salamanders come in many sizes. Most are 6 inches (15 cm) or smaller. But one type can grow to be 6 feet (1.8 m) long!

Chinese giant salamanders are the largest amphibians on Earth. They can grow to be 6 feet (1.8 m)!

Salamanders need to live near water. They live on all continents except Australia and Antarctica. They live in cooler areas. Forests and caves are good **habitats** for salamanders. Only one type of salamander lives in a desert. It sleeps for nine months and comes out when it rains.

Most salamanders lay eggs in water. Baby salamanders are born without legs. They live in the water. They leave the water when their legs grow.

Salamander eggs look like clear jelly.

Salamanders come awake at night. They eat bugs and worms. Larger salamanders might eat fish. Salamanders stay in dark places during the day.

What's the Difference?

Lizards and salamanders are different. Lizards are reptiles. Salamanders are amphibians. Lizards have dry, rough scales. They have sharp claws. Salamanders have wet skin and no scales. They do not have claws.

Unlike most salamanders, lizards can live in very dry places.

Lizards and salamanders are awake at different times. Lizards hunt during the day. Salamanders wait until night.

Salamanders and lizards can look alike in some ways. But they are very different animals!

LIZARDS

Can be many different sizes

Claws on feet

Scales

- Reptiles
- Bury their eggs
- Awake during the day

SALAMANDERS

No claws

Most are 6 inches (15 cm) or smaller

Wet bodies

- Amphibians
- Lay eggs in water
- Awake at night

GLOSSARY

amphibians (am-FIB-ee-uhnz) Amphibians are cold-blooded animals that live the first part of their life in the water and move to land as an adult. Salamanders are amphibians.

cold-blooded (KOLD-BLUD-ed) A cold-blooded animal cannot control its own body temperature and has to use the sun to keep warm. Both lizards and salamanders are cold-blooded creatures.

continent (KON-tuh-nent) A continent is one of Earth's seven largest pieces of land. Antarctica is the only continent without lizards.

habitats (HAB-ih-tats) Habitats are the places an animal can live. Salamanders need wet habitats.

reptiles (REP-tylz) Reptiles are scaly, cold-blooded animals that lay eggs. Lizards are reptiles.

TO LEARN MORE

IN THE LIBRARY

Dowling, Lucy. *Reptiles & Amphibians*. New York, NY: Windmill Books, 2015.

Pope, Kristen. *Salamanders*. Mankato, MN: The Child's World, 2016.

Rajczak Nelson, Kristen. *Amphibians*. New York, NY: Enslow Publishing, 2019.

ON THE WEB

Visit our website for links about lizards and salamanders:
childsworld.com/links

*Note to Parents, Teachers, and Librarians: We routinely verify our Web links to make sure
they are safe and active sites. So encourage your readers to check them out!*

ACTIVITY

Draw a picture of a lizard and a salamander. Your picture should clearly show the
differences between the lizard and the salamander.
Look at pages 20 and 21 for help.

INDEX